The Adventures of Robin Hood

Illustrated Classics

The Adventures of ROBIN HOOD

By Howard Pyle

Retold for young readers
by D.J. Arneson

Illustrated by Eva Clift

1 ROBIN FORMS HIS BAND

In merry old England during the time of good King Henry the Second, a famous outlaw named Robin Hood lived near the town of Nottingham. He was the finest archer in the land and dwelled in the depths of Sherwood Forest with his merry band of men. One hundred and forty strong, they were outlaws who lived a carefree life hunting the King's deer, competing against one another in archery contests, and staging mock fights with stout cudgels. Robin and his men were beloved by the people because they never turned down anyone who needed help.

Robin was not always an outlaw. One bright morning in the month of May, when he was a lad of 18, his life was changed forever.

The sun had just risen. Robin was on his way from Locksley Town to Nottingham to enter an archery contest proclaimed by the Sheriff of Nottingham. He walked along a forest path whistling a tune, with a stout bow of yew wood and a quiver filled with yard-long arrows on his back. As he rounded a turn, he met a group of foresters feasting and drinking in the shade of a tree.

"Hello, little lad with the penny bow and four for a penny arrows," a forester called with a mocking laugh. "Where might you be going?"

Robin's face reddened. He shook his bow at the men. "My bow and my arrows are as good as any of yours," he said angrily. "As for where I go, I am off to Nottingham Town to compete for the prize offered by our good sheriff."

"Listen to this lad," the forester said. "He is still wet behind the ears, yet he says he will shoot against good stout men. Ho! I doubt if he can pull a real archer's bow."

"I'll bet 20 silver coins I can hit a mark at 100 yards," Robin shot back.

The forester stepped forward. "Well boasted, little lad, but you know there is no target to make your wager."

"Give him a cup of milk and send him on his way," another said.

Robin's anger grew. He scanned the woods for a target. A herd of deer grazing in a clearing 100 yards away caught his eye . "Hark! I have found my target," he exclaimed. " I will drop the finest stag."

The forester who chided Robin put his hand on his purse. "Done!" he shouted. "Here are 20 coins that say you'll miss."

Robin placed the tip of his bow against his foot and bent it sharply to string it. He took a

Robin raised his bow.

long arrow from his quiver and fit it to his bow. He raised the bow and drew the gray goose feather to his ear. The string sang as the arrow flew as straight as a sparrow hawk to its target. The largest stag in the herd fell to the ground with Robin's arrow in its chest. "Ha!" Robin crowed, "I'll take that purse now."

The foresters were stunned. Instead of praise, they heaped scorn on the young bowman. The man who accepted Robin's bet was angry. "I'll beat your hide before I give you my purse," he said, waving a stout cudgel. "Now get out of here before we're all upon you."

"You've killed one of the king's deer," another forester said. "That's against the law."

"Catch him!" shouted a third. "We'll see he gets his ears clipped for what he's done."

"Let him go," said another. "He's only a lad."

Robin glared at the men but said nothing. His anger burned hot beneath his tunic and it was everything he could do to control it. He turned his back on the foresters and started down the path.

The forester who lost the bet was humiliated. He strung his bow and fit an arrow to it. "Let this hurry you along, little lad," he cried. He drew the string and shot.

The arrow whistled past Robin's ear. If the man had not drunk so much wine, it would have hit him. Robin spun on his heels. He drew his own bow and sent an arrow back in return. "If you think I'm not an archer, think again," he shouted.

The arrow went straight to its mark. The forester fell with a cry and lay still. When the others looked up from their fallen comrade, Robin was gone. A few men ran after him but quickly changed their minds when they realized they might meet the dead man's fate.

Robin raced through the greenwood. His joy was turned to sorrow and his heart was sick because he had killed a man. "Why did I pass this way?" he cried, blaming himself for the tragedy. "I would rather cut off my own finger than have this happen." He slowed to a walk and covered his face with his hand. When he took it away, he felt changed. "What is done is done," he said calmly. "A broken egg cannot be mended." He turned his back on Nottingham Town. His youth was behind him. His future was set.

A 200 pound reward was put on Robin's head for killing the forester and poaching the king's deer. He was outlawed and forced to live like a fugitive in the forest. He would never again enjoy happy days with his young friends of Locksley Town. The Sheriff of Nottingham vowed to bring Robin Hood to the king's court for justice. He wanted the reward for himself, but he also wanted revenge because the slain

"What is done is done," Robin said calmly.

forester was his relative.

Robin hid in Sherwood Forest for a year. He was joined by over 100 men escaping wrong and oppression. Some had poached deer to keep from starving, others had their land taken by the king, and some had been cheated by the rich and powerful. The outlaw band chose Robin as its leader. They vowed to return the high taxes, excessive rents, and wrongful fines taken from the poor by greedy barons, knights, and squires. They pledged to undo injustice and never to harm women or children. People soon realized that Robin and his merry men were not a danger, but were like themselves.

One morning Robin spoke to his men as they sat beneath the giant oak in the center of their camp. "We have had no sport for two weeks," he said, "so I am off to find adventure." He patted a small bugle tied to his belt. "If I should find it and need your help, listen for three blasts on my horn and come quickly." He turned away with a wave of his hand and stepped into the deep forest.

Robin soon reached the edge of Sherwood Forest. He wandered over the paths and byways skirting the dense woods, looking on all sides for adventure. A fair lass returned his "hello" with a smile. A fat monk rode by on a donkey. A matron passed by and he greeted a gallant knight in armor. The paths were busy with people going to and fro, but none carried adventure. He turned to a less travelled path.

"I am off to find adventure."

At a narrow bridge over a bubbling stream, he spied a tall stranger approaching from the opposite side. The two men quickened their steps to be the first to cross the bridge.

"Stand back," Robin called, "and let the better man cross first."

"Then it is you who must stand back," the tall stranger answered, "for I am the better man."

"We will see about that," Robin said, sensing adventure. "Stay where you are or I will place a shaft betwixt your ribs."

"If you dare to touch the string of your bow, I will tan your hide six shades of black and blue," the stranger said.

"Not likely," Robin replied. "My shaft would pierce your heart before you could say 'good day.' "

"A coward's speech," the stranger said. "You have a good yew bow while I have nothing but this staff." He raised the long blackthorn rod he carried and shook it boldly at Robin.

"I have never been called a coward in my life," Robin shouted. "I will put down my bow and cut a staff for myself that will settle the matter quickly." He laid his bow on the ground and stepped into a thicket alongside the path. He cut a stout oak sapling and trimmed the branches with his knife. As he trimmed, he studied the stranger. Robin was six feet tall,

but the stranger was seven. Robin's back was broad, but the stranger's was broader. Robin's chest was bold, but the stranger's bolder. "He is a giant by every measure," Robin thought. "But still I will beat his hide with this staff."

Robin returned to the path. "Here is my staff, good fellow," he called. "Prepare to feel its wrath upon thy back." He stepped onto the bridge. The stranger did the same. "We will fight until one has knocked the other into the stream," Robin said.

"Done," the stranger replied. He advanced with his staff held by both hands across his chest.

The two met in the middle of the bridge. Robin moved forward and then stepped back to draw the man off guard. The stranger was not tricked. Robin advanced again, but this time he laid a clout to the side of the stranger's head that would have toppled a mule. The man stood firm and parried Robin's blow with one of his own. Robin ducked as the staff sizzled through the air where his head had been.

The two fought until every inch of their bodies was bruised and sore. Neither budged an inch or cried out "Enough!" The glen echoed with the thunder of colliding staffs. Then Robin saw an opening. He thrust forward and laid a blow against the stranger's ribs that made his jacket smoke. The man reeled backwards to within an inch of falling into the rushing water, but recovered in time to ward off the finishing blow. He twirled his staff above his head and drove it home with such strength and speed it sent Robin flying into the stream.

The stranger slapped his side and roared with laughter. "What say you now, good lad?" he asked.

"I am floating to sea on the tide," Robin answered with a laugh. He got to his feet and splashed to the bank. "Give me your hand," he said, extending his hand to the stranger.

The tall man helped Robin onto dry ground. They eyed one another from head to foot. "There is no man between here and Canterbury who could do that to me," Robin said, shaking the water from his hair.

The tall man helped
Robin onto dry ground.

15

Robin put his horn to his lips.

"And you have taken a beating that would fell a tree," the stranger said.

Robin put his horn to his lips and blew three short blasts. Within minutes, twenty strong men dressed in Lincoln green burst from the bushes with Will Stutely in the lead.

"What has happened, Robin?" Will asked. "You are drenched."

"And drubbed besides," Robin answered, pointing to the tall stranger, "and he is the fellow who did it."

Will raised his staff. "Then he shall be drubbed and ducked as well," he shouted. "Have at him, lads!"

Before Robin could speak, Will and the others leaped on the stranger with their staffs whirling. But the tall man held them off until he was overwhelmed by their number.

"Stop!" Robin shouted. "He is a good man

who beat me fair." He turned to the stranger. "Join us," he said. "Come live in Sherwood as one of my band. You will receive three suits of Lincoln green each year, forty coins of silver, and share in the good we gain. You will be my right-hand man. What say you?"

The stranger rubbed his chin. "I have no mind to join any band that can't best me with a cudgel or bow," he said. "Yet, if any of you can shoot an arrow better than I, then I will think about joining you."

Robin's grin vanished. "You are quite sure of yourself, sir. To any other man I would say you are no longer welcome to join us. But I will stoop to you as I have never stooped to anyone." He turned to Will Stutely. "Cut a square of white bark four inches on a side," he said. "Fix it to that distant oak tree."

Will Stutely did as Robin said. The small white square was so far away it was nearly invisible. Robin spoke to the stranger. "Now, sir, if you call yourself an archer, hit that target if you can."

The stranger said nothing. He took a long arrow tufted with gray goose feathers and fit it to a stout bow. As Robin's band of men stood by, he raised the bow and drew the string to his ear. The arrow sped straight to the target. A man ran to the oak. "It is in the very center," he called. Robin's men shouted approval.

"You shot well," Robin said calmly. "Now it is my turn." He raised his bow and using his greatest skill, let the arrow fly. It flew so true it hit the end of the stranger's arrow and split it down the middle.

"By the saints!" the stranger cried. "That is the best shot I have seen in my life!" He grasped Robin's arm. "You ask would I be your man, sir? My answer is yes!"

"Then I have gained a right good man," Robin exclaimed. "What is your name,?"

"John Little," the stranger said.

Will Stutely stepped forward. "I propose a new name, sir." He filled a cap with water from the stream and poured it over the stranger's head. "From henceforth, I christen thee Little John."

The men burst into laughter. "So be it," the stranger said with a bright grin.

The men returned to their camp. They dressed Little John in a suit of Lincoln green, gave him a stout bow, and welcomed him into their merry band.

2 THE SHOOTING MATCH

The Sheriff of Nottingham was determined to capture Robin and bring him to justice. He offered 80 gold coins to anyone who would serve a warrant for the outlaw's arrest. Everyone refused. "Are the men of Nottingham cowards?" the sheriff asked.

"Robin Hood has a force of men who would break anyone's bones who dared serve a warrant on their leader," one of the sheriff's men said.

"I'll find someone else," the sheriff said. He instructed a messenger to find someone to serve the warrant.

The messenger got as far as the Blue Boar Inn. A merry crowd of the king's foresters, some friars, and a tinker filled the place. The messenger joined them. He told how Robin Hood was an outlaw and that he was looking for someone brave enough to serve an arrest warrant.

"I've not heard of this Robin Hood," the tinker said. "If he is strong, I am stronger. If he is sly, I am slyer. And if he needs arresting, I shall serve the warrant."

The messenger was relieved to find the

"I've not heard of this Robin Hood," the tinker said.

tinker and the tinker was eager to meet Robin Hood so he could collect the reward.

The next day, Robin Hood was strolling merrily down a shady lane on the road to Nottingham. The tinker approached him from the opposite direction. The tinker was singing.

"Hello!" Robin called to the tinker.

The tinker did not answer.

"Hello!" Robin called again.

"Don't interrupt a man who is singing," the tinker said curtly.

Robin eyed the man. "I say hello to be your friend," he said with a grin. "Come with me to the Blue Boar and I shall prove it with a glass of ale."

The tinker tossed his bag and hammer over his shoulder. "Spoken like a true friend," he said. They walked side by side to the Blue Boar and sat at a table across from one another.

"What is your business?" Robin asked.

The tinker leaned forward. "I carry a warrant to serve on the outlaw called Robin Hood," he whispered. "When I meet him I shall beat him 'til he begs me to give it to him."

"Ho!" exclaimed Robin, "I should like to be there." He beckoned to the innkeeper. "Bring my friend more ale," he said. "Bring as many as he likes."

The tinker drank with gusto. Soon his head was spinning. He lay his forehead on his

arm and quickly fell asleep.

Robin took the warrant from the tinker's bag. He paid the innkeeper. "I have paid in full," he said with a laugh, "but when my new friend awakes, you may charge him again. It will serve him for trying to outfox a fox."

A short while later the tinker met Robin for the second time. "Just the scoundrel I seek," the tinker said angrily. He raised his staff. "Prepare to feel my fury." He leaped forward with his staff spinning.

Robin parried the blow and answered with one of his own. The two fought long and hard, but the tinker was no match for Robin. But just when Robin moved to finish the man, his staff snapped in half. The tinker leaped at Robin and knocked him to the ground. "Now I have you," the tinker crowed. "Beg for mercy or

"Beg for mercy or suffer a cracked skull."

suffer a cracked skull."

"I am down, but not beaten," Robin replied. He blew a quick blast on his bugle horn and within moments Little John and six of his band emerged from the dark woods.

"Shall we finish this fellow?" Little John asked.

"No," Robin said. "He is a good man who belongs with us, not against us. What say you, tinker. Will you join our band?"

The tinker put out his hand. "I shall indeed," he exclaimed. "I love a merry life and will be pleased to go with you."

The people of the countryside made fun of the sheriff when they heard he could not serve a warrant on Robin Hood. The sheriff was infuriated. He rode to London Town to seek the king's help.

The sheriff was taken to the king's court which was filled with brave knights, fair ladies and elegant courtiers in service of the king. King Henry and Queen Eleanor sat amid regal splendor. The sheriff bowed deeply. "What can I do for you?" the king asked.

The sheriff told the story of Robin Hood. He explained how the outlaw band was killing the king's deer and stealing from the king's subjects. He told how Robin stole the king's own warrant before it could be served.

"What manner of sheriff can't catch a band of thieves?" the king asked angrily. "You have a force of men-at-arms and these outlaws don't even wear armor." The king pointed to the door. "If you are my sheriff, do your work. If you

The sheriff rode to London Town to seek the king's help.

fail, you are no sheriff of mine."

The sheriff was upset. He rode home in silence. Suddenly he shouted, "I have a plan!" and galloped back to Nottingham where he gathered his men. "I shall proclaim an archery contest," he said. "I will offer a huge prize. Robin Hood will enter and when he reveals himself, I will take him!"

The sheriff's messengers announced the contest all over the countryside. Anyone who could draw a long bow could enter. The prize would be a pure gold arrow.

Robin heard of the contest and was eager to enter. But one of his band spoke up. "I heard at the Blue Boar that the contest is a trap for you."

"How so?" Robin asked.

"The moment you reveal yourself, the sheriff will arrest you," the man replied.

Robin thought for a moment. "Then here is my plan," he said with a laugh to his band. "We

The sheriff had a plan.

28

shall go in disguise. Some will dress as friars, others as peasants, and some as beggars. Each will carry his bow or sword in case it is needed." He put his hand on his chest. "I will enter in disguise and shoot for the prized golden arrow."

The men roared with hearty approval.

Nottingham was filled with people on the day of the shooting match. Knights and ladies, squires and dames, and rich citizens and their wives joined the simple folk and poor peasants of the countryside, but they did not mingle. The noble and wealthy sat on a raised platform decked with flying banners, streaming scarves, and garlands of flowers near the target. The peasants sat on the grass at the opposite end of the shooting range. Ale flowed freely and everyone spoke of who would win the prize. The best archers in all of England were present, including the sheriff's own archer, Gill o' the Red Cap.

When the benches and fields were filled with spectators, the sheriff and his lady arrived. The sheriff sat stiffly on a milk-white horse, his lady on a brown filly at his side. The sheriff had a heavy gold chain around his neck. His lady's velvet gown was trimmed with swan's down. They rode like royalty to their place in the viewing stand. When they were seated, the contest began.

In the first round, all contestants would

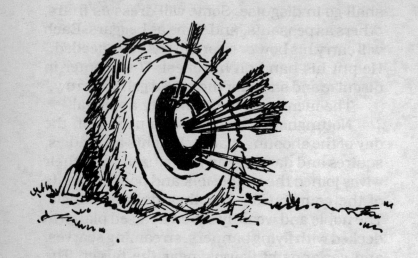

shoot one arrow at a target 150 yards away. The ten best shots in the first round would each shoot two arrows in the second round. The three best archers in that round would shoot three arrows in the third and last round. The best shot in the third round would win the prize.

The sheriff looked for Robin among the archers but nobody wore Lincoln green. "He is sure to be here even though I don't see him," he said to his lady. "He will surely be among the ten who remain after the first round."

The archers stepped to the line, one at a time, and fired their best shot at the target. At the end of the first round, six arrows were in the center and four were in the black ring. The sheriff recognized six men because they were the finest archers in the realm. Two others were from Yorkshire, another was a tall stranger in blue, and the last was a man in a tattered scarlet outfit and a patch over one eye.

"Is one of those ten Robin Hood?" the sheriff asked a man-at-arms.

"I don't know," the man said. "Six I know by sight, the tall man is too tall and the short man too short. As for the beggar in scarlet, he is blind in one eye and his beard is brown while Robin's is gold."

The sheriff smacked his fist into his open palm. "Then he is afraid to enter," he said. He was bitterly disappointed.

The contest resumed and each archer shot two more arrows. When the round was finished, the crowd roared its approval for such excellent archery. At last, only three archers remained. One was Gill o' the Red Cap, the second was the one-eyed stranger in scarlet, and the third was Adam o' the Dell of Tamworth. The crowd shouted hurrahs for the sheriff's archer and Dell of Tamworth, but nobody cheered the ragged beggar.

"Shoot well, Gill," the sheriff shouted to his man. "If you win, I'll add 100 silver coins to your prize."

Gill o' the Red Cap nodded. "I will do my best, sir," he said. He fitted an arrow to his

31

The one-eyed beggar let an arrow fly.

bowstring and drew the cord to his ear. The arrow sped like the wind to the target and struck within an inch of the center. The crowd shouted approval.

Next, the one-eyed beggar raised his bow and let an arrow fly in the time most men would still be drawing the string. It struck the target one-half inch closer to the target than Gill o' the Red Cap's shot.

The last to shoot was Adam o' the Dell. His arrow lodged alongside the beggar's.

Each of the three shot a second arrow. One shot remained for each man. Gill o' the Red Cap took careful aim and let fly. It hit a pea's width from dead center.

The crowd turned its gaze back to the shooting line where the beggar prepared his final arrow. The bowstring buzzed and the shaft flew like lightning to the target. The arrow nipped a bit of feather from Gill o' the Red Cap's arrow and slid along its side to land in the absolute center.

When Adam o' the Dell saw the stranger's perfect shot, he put down his own bow. "There is none better," he said. "He has won over us all."

The sheriff walked to the shooting line where the stranger in red leaned casually against his bow. "What are you called?" the sheriff asked.

The stranger glanced up. "I am Jock o' Teviotdale," he said.

The sheriff extended the prized gold arrow to the stranger. "You are the finest archer I have ever seen, Jock," he said. "Even better

than the coward Robin Hood who dared not show his face today. I would like you to join my service. What say you?"

"I am my own master," the stranger said, "And so I shall remain."

The sheriff was angered. "Then begone," he said. He turned on his heels and strode away.

That evening, deep in Sherwood Forest, Robin's Lincoln green-clad men gathered about a fellow dressed in bright scarlet. The stranger stripped off his red tunic and tore away the patch covering his eye. He threw them to the ground with a merry laugh. With a shout he raised the gold arrow. "I am a better shot than the coward, Robin Hood," Robin crowed, for he had beat the sheriff at his own game. He beckoned to Will Stutely and Little John. "Come with me, lads," he said. "I have a message for our fat sheriff."

That evening the sheriff sat at his table in the great hall of his house in Nottingham. His servants and men-at-arms were seated at long tables filled with food and drink. The sheriff raised his arm for silence. "I have bested that knave, Robin Hood," he said. "By not coming to the game today, he has shown his cowardice. Join me in a toast to…"

A loud thump interrupted the sheriff's speech. An arrow had flown through a window

A loud thump interrupted the sheriff's speech.

and stuck in the table in front of him. A small scroll was tied to its shaft. The sheriff opened it and read:

> "Now heaven bless thy grace this day,
>   Say all in sweet Sherwood,
> For thou didst give the prize away
>   To merry Robin Hood."

The sheriff sat heavily in his chair and covered his face with his hands. Now he knew the stranger in red was his sworn enemy, Robin Hood.

3 WILL STUTELY IS RESCUED

The sheriff was angry that he could not capture Robin Hood. He had failed to serve the king's warrant and then failed to trick Robin at the shooting match. "There is nothing left but force of arms," he thought.

The sheriff called his constables and told them his new plan. "Go into Sherwood Forest in groups of five," he instructed. "Lay in wait for Robin Hood. If any group is outnumbered by Robin's band, blow a blast on your horn. The other men will rush to your aid. The first to meet Robin Hood and bring him to me dead or alive shall receive 100 pounds of good silver money."

Sixty groups of constables, 300 men in all, poured into Sherwood Forest to find Robin and claim the reward.

The trusty innkeeper at the Blue Boar warned Robin of the sheriff's plan.

"I killed a man once," Robin told his merry men when he heard he was being hunted. "I never want to be forced to do it again. We will hide until the hunt is over."

"The sheriff will think we are cowards," a

man shouted.

"Better to hide than to kill someone," Robin replied.

The men grumbled, but they swallowed their pride and obeyed their leader.

The sheriff's men searched the forest for seven days and seven nights but nobody laid eyes on anyone wearing Lincoln green.

On the eighth day, Robin was curious to know the whereabouts of the sheriff's men. He called Will Stutely to his side. "We can't hide forever," he said to Will. "Bring me news of the hunters."

Will disguised himself in a brown friar's robe. He pulled the hood over his head to hide his face and set out for the Blue Boar. A group of the sheriff's men were there. Will sat on a

Will disguised himself in a brown friar's robe.

bench across from the men and bowed his head as if he were praying. He listened to the men's loose talk. The inn's big house cat brushed against his robe and pushed it away from his leg. A flash of Lincoln green gave him away.

A constable leaped to his feet and drew his sword. Will drew his own and the two fought a fevered duel, but the rest of the sheriff's men quickly surrounded him. They grabbed the valiant swordsman and tied him up.

Robin was resting beneath a giant greenwood tree in Sherwood when he heard shouting. Two of his yeomen and the maid from the Blue Boar ran toward him.

"Will Stutely has been captured!" a yeomen shouted.

"I saw it all!" the maid added.

"They are going to hang him tomorrow," shouted the second yeoman.

Robin raised his bugle. Before putting it to his lips, he narrowed his eyes and lowered his voice. "He shall not be hanged tomorrow," he swore. Then he blew three loud blasts.

Instantly, the woods echoed with the sound of running feet and eager voices. Robin's band gathered about their chief.

"Hark you all," Robin said. "The sheriff has captured Will and vows he will hang him tomorrow. What say you?"

Robin's band gathered about their chief.

"Never!" the men shouted. Their voices rolled to the very edge of the giant forest and rumbled back like thunder.

The next day, small groups of men emerged from the forest near Nottingham Town and assembled in a quiet dell. They were Robin's merry men and had come from different directions to avoid detection. "We will go straightaway to Nottingham Town," Robin said. "We will mix with the crowds so none will know our presence. Keep one another in sight, and do not strike if it can be avoided."

A bugle blast from a castle tower signalled Will Stutely's hanging would take place soon. Nottingham's streets were filled with people heading to the square where the famous outlaw would meet the rope. Robin and his men joined the throng.

A squad of men-at-arms entered the square with the sheriff, in shining linked chain armor, behind them on a magnificent horse. A wooden cart bearing Will Stutely followed. Will searched the crowd for faces he knew, but there were non. His heart sank. Then he raised his head. "Give me a sword so I can die like a man," he said to the sheriff."

The sheriff shook his fist. "No sword," he said. "Your fate is the rope."

"Coward!" Will shouted at the sheriff. "When my chief hears of this, you will pay dearly for

A wooden cart bearing Will Stutely entered the square.

what you do to me."

The sheriff spurred his horse and rode away.

The cart forced its way through the throng to the gallows. When it stopped, Will's heart leaped. He saw a face he knew and then another. He knew at once that the crowd was as full of his companions as a pudding has raisins.

"Stand back!" the sheriff ordered.

Little John raised himself to his full height. He swung his elbow sharply and knocked one of the sheriff's men to the ground. He pushed his way to the cart. "I think now is the time to leave your new friends, Will," he said with a grin. He cut Will's bonds with a smart stroke of his sword .

The sheriff saw the commotion. "I know that man," he shouted. "Take him!" He spurred his horse through the crowd with his sword raised and struck, but Little John ducked under the horse's belly.

"I must borrow that sword for a good cause," Little John laughed. He wrested the sword from the sheriff's grip and threw it to Will Stutely.

The square filled with shouts and the sounds of steel against steel. Robin and his men flew from the crowd like bats from a cave. The sheriff's men turned tail as a shower of arrows from the outlaws' bows descended upon them. The battle ended as quickly as it began.

Robin drew his band around him with Will Stutely in the middle. "Now that we have you back, we intend to keep you," Robin said.

"I tried to catch Robin three times," the sheriff moaned in the safety of his castle, "and each time I failed." Bitter, angry, and deeply embarrassed, he hid for many days and refused to show his face.

4 ROBIN BECOMES A BUTCHER

For almost a year Robin and his band lived peacefully in the forest. Occasionally they waylaid a rich baron or a fat squire whom they first treated with a feast before taking their purses. But after a while, Robin grew bored. He decided to avenge the sheriff's efforts to capture him.

One day, he chanced upon a butcher on his way to market. "Where might you be going?" Robin asked.

"To sell my beef and mutton at the market at Nottingham," the man replied.

A sly smile crossed Robin's face as a plan leaped into his head like a stroke of lightning. "And what do you charge for your meat, horse, and cart?" he asked.

The butcher studied his wares. "Four marks," he replied.

Robin plucked his purse from his belt and tossed it to the surprised butcher. "Here are six marks," he said. "I will buy everything so I can be a butcher for a day."

The butcher was overjoyed to sell everything at once. "I wish you well, my honest fellow," he said.

"Your well wishes I will accept," Robin said, "but few men would call me honest." He put on the butcher's apron and climbed into the cart.

Robin drove to the square in Nottingham and set up his stand. When everything was arranged, he pounded his cleaver on the table to attract attention and sang:

"Now come ye lasses, and come ye dames,
and buy your meat from me;
For three pennysworth of meat I sell
for the charge of one penny."

People hurried to the stand in amazement. Nobody had heard of three pennysworth of meat for a penny. Soon Robin's stand was empty but the nearby butchers were unable to sell a thing. They were suspicious of Robin.

"He must have stolen his goods," one butcher said.

Another stepped forward. "Even a thief would not give away his meat so cheaply," he said.

"He is a wasteful son who sold his father's land for money to live a merry life," another said.

All the butchers agreed. They went to Robin's stand and began a friendly conversation.

"The sheriff has invited the Butcher's Guild to a feast, brother," a butcher said to Robin.

"Since you are one of us, you are invited as well."

The sheriff was at the Guild Hall when the butchers and Robin arrived. "That butcher sold three pennies worth of meat for a penny," one of his men whispered to the sheriff. "He sold his father's land for silver and gold and now wants to spend it."

The sheriff stroked his chin. "I have just the place for that fool's money," he said, patting his purse. "I must meet him."

The sheriff didn't recognize Robin, and soon the two were talking and laughing together like old friends. "You're an interesting fellow," the sheriff said to Robin. "I suppose you have many horned beasts and many acres of land."

"Ay, that I have," Robin said. "My brothers and I have over 500 horned beasts, but we have not been able to sell them. I have no idea how much land I have."

Robin becomes a butcher.

"You are my friend,"
the sheriff said.

The sheriff's eyes twinkled greedily. "Perhaps I can find someone to buy your cattle," he said. "How much do you ask?"

Robin thought for a moment. "Well, they are worth at least 500 pounds of silver money," he said.

The sheriff shook his head. "You are my friend," he said, "but that is more than I have. I will offer you 300 in gold and silver for all of them."

Robin acted as if he were upset. "Now, you know they are worth over 700 pounds," he said. "Are you trying to take advantage of me?"

The sheriff looked sternly into Robin's eyes but said nothing.

Robin clapped his hand on the table. "I will accept your offer because my brothers and I need the money."

The sheriff stood. "I will have my clerk write up the papers," he said. "Then we will go to see your horned beasts."

"Do not forget to bring the money," Robin said.

A short time later, Robin and the sheriff rode side by side to Sherwood Forest. The sheriff was very pleased with himself for the bargain he made, but as they got deep into the woods, he looked nervously for signs of Robin's outlaw band. "May the saints protect us from the rogue called Robin Hood," he said.

Robin laughed. "Fear not, sheriff. I know Robin Hood and I can assure you that we are in no more danger from him than we are from me."

The sheriff wasn't pleased to hear that his companion was acquainted with the outlaw, but he said nothing.

Suddenly, a herd of the king's finest deer dashed across the path. "There are my horned beasts," Robin said. "How do you like them?"

The sheriff realized he had been tricked. He wanted no more of this false butcher. "I no longer wish your company," he said. "Go on that path and I will go on this." He turned his horse and headed out of the forest.

Robin grabbed the sheriff's horse by the reins. "No, my friend," he said, "I want you to stay." He blew three merry notes on his bugle. Seconds later, Little John appeared with a hundred men at his side.

"What have you, good master?" Little John asked.

"I have a guest to our feast," Robin replied. "He is our own sheriff ."

Robin's men doffed their hats and bowed deeply, pretending great respect, and then lined up behind Robin, Little John, and the sheriff and marched deep into the greenwood. When they reached the spreading branches of

Robin's men doffed their hats and bowed deeply.

their noble oak tree, Robin ordered the feast to begin. "Bring the best food and drink we have for his worship, the sheriff," he said. "I was his guest in Nottingham today, and now he shall be ours."

Soon the woods filled with the sweet smells of roasting venison and other delicious foods. When the feast was ready, everyone sat beneath the majestic oak and ate heartily. The sun was almost down when the merry banquet was finished. The sheriff rose to his feet. "I thank you all for such fine food and entertainment," he said. "Your respect for me shows you respect our good king. But now I must leave before it gets dark because I would not want to get lost in this forest.

Robin stepped to the sheriff's side. "If you must go, you must," he said gracefully, "but I

Everyone sat beneath the majestic oak and ate heartily.

fear you have forgotten something. We have a rule that everyone who is entertained at this forest inn of ours must pay his just share."

The sheriff laughed nervously. "I have no quarrel with that," he said. "Such food, drink, and merry laughter is worth at least 20 pounds of silver to me."

Robin put on a face of mock seriousness. "By my faith, good sheriff, I could not charge a guest as important as you such a trifling," he said. "The king's deputy deserves a reckoning worthy of his rank." He turned to his men and winked. "And that, noble sheriff, is 300 pounds."

The men roared their approval.

The sheriff stamped his foot. "I will not pay three pounds," he shouted, "and much less will I pay 300 pounds!"

Robin moved closer and spoke gravely to the sheriff. "Think again, sheriff. There sits Will Stutely who you were about to hang," he said, pointing to Will in the crowd of men. "And there are two men who suffered wounds in a brawl at the hands of your deputies." Robin gestured toward two men with scowling faces. "Best you pay as I say, or suffer the consequences."

Little John lifted the sheriff's purse from his belt and poured out the silver and gold coins it held. "Three hundred pounds," he said when he counted the last coin. The sheriff's heart sank as he watched his money go.

Robin led the sheriff's horse to the main path. "Fare thee well, sheriff," he said. "The next time you think about cheating someone, remember this feast." He clapped his hands and the horse bolted up the path with the sheriff hanging on for his life.

5 ROBIN MEETS WILL SCARLET

Robin's band grew slowly. Arthur-a-Bland, the tanner, joined after taking a drubbing from Little John's quarterstaff. Now he was Robin's faithful companion.

One hot summer day, Robin, Little John, and the tanner were strolling the path through Sherwood. They stopped at a sparkling spring for a drink and then lay on the cool grass to rest. Robin's gaze drifted to the dusty path. A young man approached.

"He is a gaily feathered bird if ever I saw one," Robin said, remarking on the man's silk vest and stockings. A handsome sword hung at his belt in a finely tooled scabbard of leather decorated with gold thread. A thick feather that curled all the way to his shoulders hung from his scarlet red cap. He held a bright yellow rose that he sniffed as he walked. "Such a pretty fellow is a rare sight in Sherwood."

"He is too pretty for my taste," Little John said. "But he is a hearty fellow nonetheless. His shoulders are as broad as a young bull and his arms as sinewed as my own."

The tanner also studied the young man.

"With muscles like that, I think he is not the whipped-cream gallant one might think."

Robin and Little John nodded agreement.

"I wonder who he is?" Robin asked. "Judging by the color of his fair hair, I think he may be a Norman scoundrel and not a good Saxon."

"A great baron's son, no doubt," Little John answered. "I daresay his purse is filled with money."

"No doubt," Robin said. "It angers me to see such lordlings live on the ill-gotten gains of their families."

Little John shook his head. "I'm not so sure he's a Norman," he said. "He may be a good man after all."

Robin leaped to his feet. "No!" he said. "That fair lad is what I say he is. To prove it, I

"He is a gaily feathered bird," Robin said.

will take his purse to see if it holds foul money. If I am wrong, he may go on his way. But if he is a Norman with our countrymen's money in his purse, I will pluck him like a goose." He stepped out of the shade and onto the path. He spread his feet wide, put his hands on his hips and waited for the stranger.

The young man sniffed his rose, but did not look at Robin. When the two men were almost face to face, Robin tightened his grip on his quarterstaff. "Halt," he commanded.

The man looked into Robin's eyes. "I will do as you say, but only for as long as it takes you to tell me why," he said in a gentle voice. His words were much bolder than his appearance.

Robin smiled. "I only wish to know you, fair stranger," he said. "I would like to see your purse so that I can judge if you have more wealth than our law allows. Surely you know the saying, 'He who is fat from over-living should lose some weight.' "

The young man continued to sniff his rose. "I have business elsewhere," he said. "As I have done you no harm, I ask you to let me pass."

"Not until I have seen your purse," Robin said, planting his feet on the path.

"In that case, I am afraid I will have to kill you," the stranger said softly. He drew his fine sword.

Robin wagged his finger at the bold fellow.

"Put away your weapon," Robin said.

"Put away your weapon," he said. "I would easily break it in half like a barley straw with my staff. However, if it is a fight you want, cut a staff to defend yourself."

The man did as Robin said. He put away his sword and stepped into a thicket of woods. He studied the strong saplings growing there. When he found one he liked, he grasped it with his hands. Robin, Little John, and the tanner watched with amazement as he pulled the tree out by its roots.

"By heaven!" Little John exclaimed. "Our master is in for a better fight than he thought."

The stranger returned to the path with his staff. Robin did not move an inch.

The two faced off and immediately began to rattle one another with solid clouts. The woods rang with the steady sound of falling blows. Robin struck the stranger in the ribs. Rather than topple as an ordinary man would, the stranger merely countered with a harder blow to Robin's ribs. The dust of the path began to rise and soon the two men were obscured. Little John and the tanner listened to the harsh sounds of sticks and the dull thuds of well-aimed blows against flesh. The battle went back and forth with neither man gaining or losing.

Suddenly, the stranger raised his cudgel and lay a blow against Robin's staff that nearly tore it from his grip. He followed the first blow with another, and then a third. The final blow knocked Robin to the ground in a heap.

"Hold!" Robin shouted. "I yield."

Robin's cry came just in time to stop a blow that would surely have killed him.

Little John and the tanner leaped forward with their staffs poised. "Drop your staff," Little

"I am Will Gamwell."

John shouted.

The young man shook his head. "No, I will not," he said quietly. "Now come if you must, and I will take on both of you, though if you are as good as this fellow, then I will surely have my hands full." He put his staff up, ready to fight Robin's companions.

Robin jumped to his feet and leaped between the men. "Stop!" he shouted. He dusted himself off and then turned to the stranger. "Tell me your name, good fellow."

The stranger put down his staff. "I am Will Gamwell," he said. "I am here to find my mother's young brother, my uncle. He is called Robin Hood."

58

Robin's face lighted up with pride. "Ha!" he exclaimed. "Now I recognize you. But you were just a lad when I saw you last. Do you remember how I taught you to use a bow? You had the promise of a keen archer. And how I showed you to use a staff, which I can say now you learned well? Don't you know me?" he asked. "I am your uncle."

Will Gamwell blushed. "I looked up to you more than any man alive," he said. "Had I known it was you, I would not have lifted my hand against you."

Robin glanced at his companions. "You barely touched me," he said, rubbing his aching side, "but let's not talk of that. Tell me, nephew, what brings you to Sherwood in search of me?"

Will Gamwell's face saddened. "The man who supervised my father's property was an evil person," he said. "He spoke badly of my father, even though my father employed him. It troubled me to hear him speak ill. One day he harshly criticized my father and I could stand it no more. I struck the man on the ear. He fell and died of a broken neck. My mother and father packed me off to find you and escape the law."

"Then you will join my band of merry fellows and be one of us," Robin said. "But first you have to change your name." Robin studied his young nephew for a moment. "Because of your colorful clothes, you will be called Will Scarlet."

Little John put his hand out to the merry band's newest member. "The name fits you well," he said. "Your strength will be told in song and story." He turned to Robin. "Just as the story of the drubbing you gave our good master will be heard across the land."

Robin wagged his finger at Little John. "Let's keep that matter to ourselves," he said.

"But you are quick to tell how I once grew fat and lazy," Little John answered.

"I have told that story for the last time," Robin said quickly.

"Done," Little John said. "The stories are put to rest from this day on. I did not see you soundly drubbed today and I did not see you fall head over heels in the dust. If any man ever says it was so, I will correct his story with my staff."

Everyone laughed as they turned and headed into the depths of Sherwood.

6 ROBIN AND ALLAN-A-DALE

Robin was still stiff from his drubbing by Will Scarlet, but there were more important things on his mind. No strangers with fat purses had passed through Sherwood Forest for some time. "Nobody has dined with us lately," Robin said to Will Stutely as the two sat beneath the great oak. "Our purse is nearly empty. If we don't find someone to fill it, we will go hungry."

"Too true," Will Stutely answered.

"Then take six men with you and go forth to find someone," Robin said. "Bring him here and we will feast together before we lighten his purse."

Will Stutely rose to his feet. "I will do that happily," he said.

Will chose Little John, Arthur-a-Bland, and the miller, who had just joined the band. With three others, the group set out on the path to find a rich guest.

The small band searched the forest. They walked up one path and down another, but no prize came their way. "It is always thus," Will Stutely said. "When you are hunting, the deer are as rare as snow in June, but when you don't seek them, they hang about in swarms like mayflies."

Soon it was evening and Will decided to return empty-handed to the great oak. But as the men passed a thicket of bushes, they heard moaning. "Someone is in distress," Will said. He didn't like to poke his nose into things the way Robin did, but his curiosity got the best of him. "Let's see what is up."

The small band pushed aside the bushes. In a clearing near a bubbling brook sat a youth with his hands covering his face. He was weeping.

"Hello!" Will said. "And why are you killing this bright green grass with your tears?"

The youth leaped to his feet and drew his bow, fitting an arrow to the string as fast as a bat catches bugs, ready to shoot if the men came closer.

"I have seen this lad," the miller said. "He is a minstrel. Just last week I saw him laughing and singing."

"Stop sniveling, man," Will said. "Put down your bow. We mean no harm."

Will Scarlet stepped forward. He knew the youth was deeply troubled. "Don't mind these rough fellows," Will said. "They mean well. Come with us and we will learn why your song has turned to sorrow."

*"Why are you killing
this bright green grass
with your tears?"*

The youth picked up his harp and without
saying a word, accompanied the men into the
forest. Soon they came to the great oak. Large
fires lit the woods and the smell of food filled
the air. Robin greeted the new arrival. "Welcome
to our glen," he said. "Join us as our guest."

The youth stared at Robin. "You are the
great Robin Hood," he said, not believing his
eyes.

"I am called by that name," Robin replied.
"Now, I trust you have a fat purse with you."

The youth shook his head. "I have not
purse or money," he said. He put his hand into
his jacket and pulled out a coin that had been
broken in half. "All I have is this half a sixpence.
The other half is in the hands of the one I love."

Robin was dismayed because he hoped for
gold and silver. But his face warmed at the
sight of the sad youth with tears in his eyes.
"Cheer up, lad. I don't know your problem, but

it can't be as bad as it seems. Tell us who you are and what you are up to."

The youth sat beneath the great oak and the others gathered around him. "I am Allan-a-Dale, good master," he said. "I am 20 years old and a minstrel."

"I know you now," Robin said. "Go on with your story."

The young minstrel sighed deeply. "I was travelling the countryside, singing for my bread and coins, when I stopped for the evening at a farmhouse for the night. There I met a maiden as beautiful as she was pure and fell in love at once. Luckily, she felt the same for me. We broke a sixpence, each vowing to be true to one another forever."

The men gathered around the youth were as silent as stones in a wall. Robin urged the youth to continue.

"When sweet Ellen o' the Dale told her father of our love, he took her away at once," Allan said sadly. "That was a month and a half ago. Then, just this morning, I heard that her father promised her in marriage to Sir Stephen of Trent, a knight of wealth and power."

"A father would think that a fine match for a daughter," Robin said. "But your love for her is greater than any man's and your story touches our hearts."

"I have a mind to take my staff to Sir

Stephen's head," Little John said. "Who does he think he is that he can choose a tender lass for a wife the way he would select a horse? Besides, he is as old as the maid's own grandfather."

"But has she not agreed?" Will Scarlet asked.

"Not at all," Allan-a-Dale answered. "It is true she will do as her father wishes, but his wishes aren't hers. If she marries Sir Stephen, her heart will break."

Robin had been silent but his quick mind was busy. Now he spoke. "Tell me, fair lad, if it were arranged properly, would your true love marry you?"

Allan leaped to his feet. "Aye, she would!" he cried.

"We broke a sixpence, each vowing to be true to one another forever."

Robin put his hand on Allan-a-Dale's shoulder. "If her father is the kind of man I think he is, when he learns his daughter has married you, he will give you both his blessing." He paused. "There is one problem," he went on. "We have no priest to perform the wedding."

"I know of a priest," Will Scarlet said. "He is the friar of Fountain Abbey. I can take you there and back in one day."

Robin turned to Allan-a-Dale who had listened with great interest. "I promise you this, young friend," he said. "In two days time you and your fair Ellen will be married. I will find this friar of Fountain Abbey tomorrow and bring him here, even if I have to urge him with my staff."

"Don't be so sure he'll come," Will Scarlet said with a grin. "He will join two lovers because his nature is good and true and he loves a feast more than most. But he has an independent way that you will learn soon enough."

The feast was ready, so without further talk of what lay ahead, the merry group joined

together in song and food until the forest rang
with their laughter. And young Allan-a-Dale,
his future brighter than ever before, sang with
them. By evening's end, he was a member of
Robin's outlaw band.

7 ROBIN SEEKS THE FRIAR OF THE FOUNTAIN

Early the next morning while the dew was still bright on the grass, Robin set forth to find the friar of the Fountain. "I will take Little John, Will Scarlet, David of Doncaster, and Arthur-a-Bland with me," he said to Will Stutely. "You guard our forest home."

Robin dressed in a fine coat of chain mail which he covered with his suit of Lincoln green. He put a steel helmet on his head, but covered it with his soft white leather hat. He hung his good broadsword at his side and was ready.

The five merry men set off to find the friar. They walked many miles, and as they paused for a rest in the shade of a tree, they heard two voices. "That is strange," Robin said, "but if that is two men conversing , they sound much alike to me." He told his men to wait while he investigated.

"You always seek adventure alone," Will Scarlet complained.

"There is no danger," he said. "Wait for me to return."

Robin disappeared into the bushes. Soon he came to a small stream. The voices came from behind a small rise. Robin lay on the grass and peered over the top. A few yards below, sitting calmly on the grass at the edge of the stream, was a short, fat fellow in a loose robe. His head was as round as a ball with a ring of curly hair and a bald spot in the center. He wore a short, curly black beard. There was only one man, but there were two voices. Robin listened.

"You are a fine fellow," the fat man said.

He changed his voice. "Thank you," he said, "and so are you."

The man changed his voice again. "May I offer you a drink of this good ale," he said in his first voice.

"Well, thank you, my dear friend, I don't mind if I do," he said in his second voice.

The man put a flask to his lips and drank

69

eagerly. "That was fine ale indeed," he said in his first voice. He put the flask into his other hand. "May I offer you a taste?"

"Indeed, you may," he said in his second voice. He took another sip, this time from the other hand.

Robin bit his lip to keep from laughing. "What a merry fellow this is," he thought.

The fat man, who by his robes and his haircut was a friar of the church, began to sing a ballad. As he finished the final verse, Robin joined in. The friar did not seem to hear Robin's voice, but the moment his song was ended, he leaped to his feet. He slapped his steel cap on his head and grabbed his broadsword from his side. "What spy have we here?" he bellowed. "Come from your hiding place and I will carve you like a turkey." He waved his stout sword in the air.

Robin rose and walked down the hill with a cheerful step. "Put away that toothpick," he said. "Men who sing so well together should not quarrel." Then, spying the flask in the friar's left hand, asked, "Is that ale by any chance? My throat is as parched as dust."

The friar looked glum. "You ask for drink even though I have not invited you," he said. "However, I am a good man and would not refuse a thirsty man." He handed the flask to Robin who drank heartily.

"Is that ale by any chance?"

When he was finished, Robin returned the flask. "Do you know this countryside?" Robin asked.

The friar nodded that he did.

"Then perhaps you can direct me to a place called Fountain Abbey. I seek its friar," Robin said. "I don't know if he is to be found on this side of the stream or the other."

"Perhaps you should look for yourself," the friar said.

Robin pointed to his clothes. "I would like to cross, but I do not want to get my clothes wet," he said. He eyed the friar. "Since your back is broad and your legs stout, I would like you to carry me to the other side."

The friar turned as red as a rose. "By the saints!" he exclaimed. "You are asking me, holy Tuck, to carry you?" As suddenly as it appeared, the friar's anger vanished. "Well,

71

why shouldn't I," he said quietly. "Saint Christopher carried a stranger across a river, so I can do the same."

The two stepped to the river's bank. The friar tucked his robes up so his knees showed. He put his sword under his arm. "Perhaps I should carry your sword as well," he said to Robin. "It is the least I can do."

Robin paused, but then gave the fat friar his broadsword. He clambered onto the man's back and soon the two were on the other side. Robin put his hand out. "Thank you, good friend," he said. "And now if I may have my sword, I shall be on my way."

The friar grinned broadly. "On your way, perhaps," he said, "but first, I have a favor to ask." His grin slipped from his face as quickly as if it were a mask. He took his sword and pointed it at Robin's chin. "Since I am now on the wrong side of the river, I will have you carry me to the other side."

"You are a cunning fellow," Robin said. "I was deceived to think you were a holy man, which clearly you aren't."

"Speak not of hoodwinking," the friar said, brandishing his sword, "or you'll feel the touch of blue steel."

"I will do as you say," Robin said, "but first return my sword. I promise not to use it against you."

"It makes no difference," the friar said, "I am not afraid of you with or without a blade." He handed Robin the sword. "Now carry me back to my side of the river."

Robin bent down so the man could cling to his back. He stumbled over the stones as he carried the heavy friar toward the opposite bank. The friar clung tightly to keep from falling, but Robin's arms were free. He reached behind him and loosened the friar's belt. The moment they reached dry land and the friar was on his own two feet, Robin grabbed the

man's belt. It came off in his hand and with it the friar's sword.

"Now I have you," Robin said. He put the point of the sword under the friar's thick jowls. "You are daring and worthy, but I have better things to do. I must reach the other side of this river high and dry, so once more I bid you to carry me."

The friar realized he had no choice. "Again, I will do it," he said grimly. "Now return my sword for I promise not to use it."

Robin gave the friar the sword and climbed on his back for the second time. The friar stepped into the water. When he was in the very middle, he stopped. He bucked suddenly and Robin flew from his back as easily as if he had been a sack of grain. He fell into the water

The friar bucked suddenly.

with a mighty splash.

"Now cool that hot spirit of yours before serious trouble gets you," the friar said. He walked back to the river bank he had just left.

Robin shook himself and splashed to the same side as the friar. "Trouble has found you first," he shouted. With that he drew his sword.

The friar already had his sword in his hand. Instantly the two men clashed. The ringing of steel and the clang of sword against armor filled the air. It was a fight in earnest, and if each were not armored, blood would have flowed. The two swordsmen thrust and parried but neither gained on the other because they were equally good. At last Robin dropped his sword arm. "Hold your sword, good friend," he said.

The friar also put his sword down. "What now?" he asked.

"Just permit me to blow three blasts on my

bugle horn," Robin said.

"If it is a trick, I still am not afraid of you," the friar answered. "But you must let me blow this whistle three times, too."

"Done," Robin said, and putting his bugle to his lips, he blew three short blasts.

At the same time the friar blew three quick squeaks on his whistle.

The echoes had not died before the woods were filled with noise. From one side burst Will Scarlet and the rest of the men. From the other came the snarls of four sleek hounds with sharp teeth and murder in their eyes.

"A trick for a trick, my traitorous friend," the friar shouted. "At him, Beauty. At him, Fang!" He ordered the dogs to attack Robin.

Robin took one look at the glistening teeth and unblinking gray eyes of the beasts and headed for the nearest tree. He dropped his sword and clambered to safety, seconds before the first beast was nipping at his shadow.

Robin's men saw their master's plight. All but Will Scarlet drew their bows and sent arrows flying. The dogs leaped at the last instant, and none were hit. Will Scarlet stepped forward. "Down, Fang! Down, Beauty!" he shouted at the dogs, calling each by its name.

The dogs shrank at the sound of Will's command.

The friar was amazed. "What is this?" he

cried. "Are you some kind of wizard who can turn a wild beast into a lamb?" But the moment Will stepped closer, the friar's eyes lighted with delight. "Will Gamwell!" he shouted. "But what are you doing in the company of men like these?"

"My name is now Will Scarlet, Tuck," Will said. "And this is my good uncle, Robin Hood."

"By the saints!" the friar exclaimed as Robin scrambled down the tree. "I have heard your praises sung, but I never thought I would meet you in battle. No wonder you put up such a good fight. Forgive me."

"I am as thankful as you, good friar," Robin said. "If Will had not called off these beasts, I dare not think of my fate."

Robin headed for the nearest tree.

Will Scarlet explained how he had joined Robin's merry band. But Robin was eager to leave.

"I must find the friar of the Fountain," Robin said.

Will laughed aloud. "Then look no farther," he said, pointing to the fat friar at his side. "This is the friar you seek."

"I am called by many names," the friar said, "but many simply call me Friar Tuck." He looked into Robin's face. "But tell me, good master, why is it you seek me?"

"Come with us to Sherwood," Robin answered, "and I will tell you."

So Friar Tuck joined the small company which quickly made its way into the depths of the forest with the fierce dogs at their heels.

8 ROBIN ARRANGES A WEDDING

The next morning Robin gathered his men. "I will take 20 men to the church where fair Ellen is to be married," he said. "Friar Tuck will join us." While his men made ready, Robin dressed in the colorful clothes of a minstrel and hung a harp over his shoulder. He handed two small bags of gold to Little John. "Keep this safe until I ask for it," he said. When all were ready, they set off for the church.

They arrived at the church before anyone else was there. "The friar of the church has arrived," a lookout said.

Robin told his men to wait until they were needed. He took Will Stutely, Little John, and Friar Tuck with him. "Talk to the old friar at the church," Robin said to Friar Tuck. "We will follow."

Friar Tuck hurried to the church and soon had the old friar in conversation. "I have heard there is to be a gay wedding today," Friar Tuck said. "I would like to sit quietly and watch if I may."

"My brothers are always welcome," the old friar said to the fat friar. "Come inside." The friars entered the church by a rear door.

In the meantime, Robin, Will Stutely, and Little John went to the front of the church. Robin, looking to all the world like a minstrel, sat by the door, but Will and Little John went inside. Little John carried the bags of gold.

A group of men on horseback approached the church. Behind them, in elegant finery and wearing a heavy gold chain around his neck, was the Bishop of Hereford. Although he was a man of the church, he acted like a rich and powerful lord, which is what he really wanted to be. The bishop was there to perform the wedding ceremony.

Robin narrowed his eyes as he studied the bishop's expensive clothes. "The money for that finery surely came from the poor," he said quietly. He tightened his grip on his harp as if it were his bow.

The Bishop of Hereford stopped at the door before entering the church. "And who is this in such colorful clothes?" he asked, studying Robin's minstrel disguise.

"I am a harpist," Robin said. "Today I will play such magic at this wedding that the fair bride will love the man she marries for the rest of their days."

The Bishop of Hereford knew that Ellen's marriage to Sir Stephan was arranged. He also knew she did not love the old man. He smiled

at Robin. "If you can do that, I will pay you a princely sum," he said. "But first, I must hear how you play."

Robin pulled away. "No, kind sir, I will play only when the time is right," he answered.

"So be it," the bishop said as the wedding party arrived. Sir Stephan, old but elegant in garments of fine silk and velvet, led the group. At his side was a stout, ordinary man, who Robin knew must be Ellen's father. Behind them, riding on a couch carried by two strong horses, was Ellen. A squad of six men-at-arms wearing flashing steel helmets and bearing stout broadswords brought up the rear.

Ellen's face was filled with sorrow. Sir Stephan took her hand and led her to the church. It was more as if he were leading her to her execution.

"This is not a fit wedding."

The Bishop of Hereford nudged Robin. "Why aren't you playing?" he asked sternly.

"The time is not right," Robin said.

As Ellen and Sir Stephan took their places in front of the bishop at the altar, Robin moved closer. He boldly stepped between the young bride and the old groom. "This is not a fit wedding," he said brashly. "This man is not this maid's true love."

Everyone was shocked. They stared dumbfounded at Robin who blew three short blasts on his bugle. Little John and Will Stutely leaped from their hiding places with their swords drawn. Friar Tuck hurried down the aisle.

Sir Stephan had regained his wits. "Down with them," he shouted to his men-at-arms.

The armed guards rushed forward with

82

drawn swords, but before they were halfway down the aisle, 18 stout men dressed in bright Lincoln green raced into the church with Allan-a-Dale in the front. He carried Robin's trusty bow and a quiver of fine arrows and handed them to his chief.

"If no man moves, no harm will come," Robin shouted. Then, turning to young Allan-a-Dale, he said, "Here is fair Ellen's true love who she will marry today."

Ellen's father stepped forward. "I am her father," he said, "and I say she will marry Sir Stephan and nobody else."

Sir Stephan had watched the whole affair quietly. Now he spoke. "No, Edward," he said, "I will not marry your daughter today or any other day. If she chooses to give up a life of riches as my wife, you may have her back. I did not know she loved this fellow. If she chooses him over me, so be it." He gathered his men and left.

Allan-a-Dale is Ellen's true love.

The bishop tried to join him. "I have no business here, either," he said.

Robin stopped him. "Stay, Lord Bishop," he said. "You will play your part yet." He turned to Ellen's father. "Give your blessing to your daughter's wedding and all will be well." He signalled to Little John who gave him the two bags of gold. Robin opened the bags. "Here are two bags of gold," he said to Ellen's father. "They are yours if you give your blessing. If you don't, the wedding will go on anyway and I will keep the gold. What say you?"

Ellen's father stared at the stone floor in deep thought and then he raised his eyes to Robin. "If that is what she wants, so be it," he said. "I thought I would make a lady of her, but if she wants to be what she wants to be, then I give her my blessing."

Friar Tuck quickly read the required wedding announcement. When he finished, he joined the two young lovers by the hands and wed them as was his right to do.

Robin beamed at the young couple and then turned to Edward. "Here is the gold as I promised," he said. Then he spun on his heels to face the bishop. Robin grasped the gold chain around the bishop's neck. "And here is the Bishop's present for the bride."

The bishop's face grew as red as the sunset, but he was surrounded by Robin's men and had no choice. He slipped the chain from his neck and handed it to Robin who draped it over Ellen's fair shoulders. "Thank you for your fine gift, Bishop," Robin said to the bishop. "And now we shall hold a wedding feast the likes of which has never been seen."

With Allan and his bride beaming with joy, Robin and his merry band hurried back to Sherwood Forest for the feast.

9 THE SHOOTING CONTEST

Robin and his men filled their days with adventure and daring. They kept their promise to right the injustices done to the poor, and their exploits gained fame throughout the land. Ordinary folks were friends to Robin Hood and his merry band, while the rich and dishonest were their enemies. The danger came from the rich and powerful who sought Robin's capture.

One balmy spring day when the flowers were in full bloom and the air was as sweet as honey, a youth riding a milk-white Barbary mare appeared on the path near Sherwood Forest. He was the queen's page, a lad of 16 named Richard Partington. He was looking for Robin.

The handsome young man reined his horse in front of the Blue Boar. Sitting in the shade of the wayside inn were five stout men. Two wore clothes of bright Lincoln green. Richard asked the innkeeper for a glass of cool drink. When it arrived, he raised the glass in a toast. "To the health and happiness of my fair queen," he said. "May her wishes come true."

"And what might the queen's wishes be?"

one of the Lincoln green-clad men asked.

"She has sent me to find a certain yeoman called Robin Hood," the page replied.

The two men in green whispered to one another. Then one spoke. "Why does she want Robin Hood?" he asked. "I know a little about him and might be able to help you."

The page's face brightened. "Take me to him if you can. It will serve him and our queen. I assure you no harm will befall him."

The two men nodded. "Come with us," one said.

Robin greeted the trio when it arrived in Sherwood. "Welcome," he said to the page, "What brings a fine lad like you to our humble forest?"

"I can see that you are Robin Hood and

*Richard Partington,
the queen's page,
was looking for Robin.*

The page gave Robin a fine gold ring.

these your merry men," the page said. "I bring greetings from our noble queen Eleanor. She wishes to meet with you in London Town. She will protect you from harm." The page caught his breath. "In four days, King Henry will hold a shooting match in Finsbury Fields. The finest archers in England will be there. The queen knows your fame and is sure that you would win. She bids you to enter the contest. As a sign of her good faith, she sends this golden ring from her own finger." The page gave Robin a finely wrought gold ring which he slipped onto his little finger.

Robin smiled. "Fair page," he said, "I will do what our queen wishes and go with you to

London Town. But first, we must feast."

While the feast was being prepared, Robin spoke to his closest men. "Little John, Will Scarlet, and Allan-a-Dale will enter the contest with me," he said. "Will Stutely will be chief while I am gone."

Three days later, on the morning of the contest, the four outlaws and the young page entered high-walled London Town.

"I will tell our queen we have arrived," Richard Partington said. He vanished through the gate of the king's towered stone castle. Moments later he beckoned Robin and his men to follow.

The queen sat on a finely decorated bench in her private room. A dozen ladies-in-waiting tended her. The queen smiled as Robin and the others entered.

Robin kneeled at the queen's feet. "I am Robin Hood," he said. "You asked me to come and I am here. I will do your bidding as a true servant, even if it means shedding my last drop of blood."

"Rise, Robin," the queen said. She gestured to a table laden with fine food and drink. "Your long journey deserves a reward. Come, we will feast and you will tell me of all your adventures."

Soon the room buzzed with stories of the merry men. Robin told of the encounter with the Bishop of Hereford and others. The queen laughed aloud at every tale. Later, Allan-a-Dale sang for her to a tune he played on his harp. Soon it was time for the contest to begin.

Finsbury Fields was ablaze with color. Streamers and banners flew from tall poles, and the booths housing the archery contestants were decorated with flags and silk. The archers had come from all over England and were the finest in the land. The king's own yeomen were among them. In all, over 800 men would vie for the prizes offered by the king. The first prize was 50 pounds of gold money, a silver bugle horn, and ten white arrows tipped with gold. Second prize was five fat deer that the winner could take whenever he wanted. The third prize was two huge barrels of the best wine.

Each archer would shoot seven arrows. The three best archers from each band would shoot again in the next round. Of these, the three best would shoot. The contest would continue until only three remained. They would shoot against one another for the three prizes.

A throng of spectators crowded along the shooting range. A hush fell over the crowd and then a loud cheer went up as the king and queen and their court arrived. The sharp trill of a bugle announced the start of the contest.

The archers lined up in ranks at the shooting line. They raised their bows as a sign of allegiance to the king. Then the shooting

began. Over five thousand arrows were fired in the first round. The judges examined the targets after each volley and determined the winners. New targets were put in place and the next round was shot. Very few archers missed the targets, but some were closer to the bull's-eye than others. Finally, only ten archers remained. They went to their tents to rest for the final round.

The queen leaned close to the king and spoke into his ear. "Do you think you have found the ten best archers in all of merry England?" she asked.

"Without a doubt," the king said. "There are none better in the whole world."

The queen smiled. "I know three who can best them all," she said. "But I will enter them only if you promise their safety."

The king laughed out loud. "Are you making a bet with me?" he asked. "If so, I promise the safety of your archers."

The queen beckoned to her page and told him to bring her archers to the field. The king's ten archers took their places on the shooting line. They placed arrows in their bows and shot as the crowd roared approval. When the targets were measured, Gilbert, Tepus, and Hubert were the the winners. They would shoot against the queen's archers.

A murmur rose from the crowd as a small group of men approached. The queen's page took them to the king and queen. The Bishop of Hereford, who stood behind the queen, recognized them at once. He started to speak but the queen nodded to him to be silent.

"This is Locksley," the queen said to King Henry as Robin bowed before him. "He and his companions will shoot against your men for the bet we have made."

Robin bowed to the queen. "I will do my best for you, or never lift a bow again," he said. With that he and the others went to the shooting line.

"Who are these fellows?" the king asked.

The bishop could not hold his tongue any longer. "They are outlaws, your majesty," he said. "They are none other than Robin Hood,

Little John, Will Scarlet, and Allan-a-Dale."

The king frowned darkly. "Is this true?" he asked the queen.

"Yes," she replied. "The bishop knows them well for he spent a merry time with Robin Hood and his band in Sherwood Forest."

The bishop blushed beet-red at the memory of how Robin took his ill-gotten treasure to share with the poor.

"So be it," the king said. "I have said they will be safe for 40 days and I will keep my word. But when the 40 days are over, this outlaw will have to be on his guard." He turned to his archers. "I will fill your caps with silver if you outshoot these fellows, but if you lose, you must give the prizes you have already won to them."

"Who are these fellows?"
the king asked.

New targets were set up and the six contestants took their places. The crowd buzzed with excitement because everyone knew of Robin and his men and how well they could shoot.

A coin was tossed to see which side would shoot first. The king's men won and Hubert was first. His three arrows fell within inches of the center. The crowd roared approval.

Next, Will Scarlet nocked his bow. He was over-cautious and his first arrow landed in the black ring. "Don't wait so long to shoot or we are in trouble," Robin said. Will nodded. He put another arrow in his bow and fired. It went straight to the center of the white circle. His third arrow did the same. But Hubert's shooting was better.

"Your outlaws will lose if that is as good as

94

they can do," the king said to Queen Eleanor.

Tepus loaded his bow and shot. He, too, took too long to fire and his first arrow hit the black ring. His second hit near the white center and the third landed directly in the middle.

"That was a fine shot, Tepus," Robin said. He nodded to Little John. "Do your best for we are against true archers."

Little John shot three arrows so quickly that the first was still quaking when the last hit the target. They fell in a tight group in the center. The crowd was dead quiet for it was the best shooting of the whole day.

Gilbert took his place. All three of his shots hit the center. Robin nodded approval. "You are as fine an archer as I have ever seen," he said.

Now it was Robin's turn. He quickly fit an arrow to his bowstring and while still talking calmly to Gilbert, fired his first shot. It struck nearly dead center. Gilbert was astounded. But Robin did not pause. He nocked another arrow and fired as quickly as he had the first. It hit his first arrow and came to a rest against it. A murmur went up from the crowd. There had never been such fine shooting in the history of the sport. The king began to squirm and his face clouded with anger. Robin raised his bow for his third shot. The arrow sped silently toward the target. It hit so close to the others that from a distance all three looked like one fat arrow in the center of the target.

Gilbert offered his hand to Robin. "You and your men have beat us fairly," he said.

The king leaped from his place. "No!" he shouted. "Gilbert has hit the center three times. The contest is not over. He and Robin Hood shall shoot again!"

A new target was put in place. Nobody dared challenge the king for they could see how upset he was.

Gilbert loaded his bow and shot. The arrow was touched by a breath of wind and fell a barley straw's width from the center.

Robin smiled. "You have left barely enough room in the center for my shaft," he said. He let his arrow fly. It sailed straight to the center of the target.

The crowd let up a loud roar of approval but the king was not happy. He rose solemnly from his place and with his queen and court following in his trail, stalked off, his heart filled with anger.

The judges stepped forward with the prizes. They gave the silver bugle, golden arrows, and 30 pounds of gold money to Robin. Robin bowed graciously. "I will accept this bugle as a remembrance of this day," he said. "But the golden arrows go to the ten best archers who shot last because they have earned them." He turned to Gilbert. "To you, the best archer in all the king's guard, I give the purse of gold money." He handed the purse to the surprised man.

Little John, who won the second prize of 100 fat deer, gave 30 to Tepus who he had beaten and the rest to the other bands of archers who had shot that day. Hubert, who shot third, was awarded the barrels of wine.

The crowd tossed their caps into the air as they cheered Robin and his men and the fine contest they had seen.

But as the happy throng milled over the fields, one of the king's guards stepped toward Robin. He pulled his sleeve. "Good master," he said, "a certain young page called Richard Partington has been searching for you but could not reach you in this crowd. He asks me to tell you this strange message: 'The lion grows. Beware thy head.'"

Robin knew at once that he was in danger. The angered King Henry would not let this day go unavenged. Robin called his men and before anyone noticed, they were gone.

10 THE CHASE OF ROBIN HOOD

Robin and his men had scarcely left Finsbury Fields for the safety of Sherwood Forest when the king changed his mind about his promise. The Bishop of Hereford was behind it. "I would not let such a prize escape if I were king," the bishop said. "I would send my men after him and rid England of this thief."

The king was upset over losing his bet to the queen. He thought about what the bishop said. "I will do it," he said. He ordered his men to find Robin.

In the meantime, Robin, Little John, Will Scarlet, and Allan trudged happily homeward, content that the king had promised their safety. By evening they were tired and hungry and stopped at an inn. As they sat at a table laden with food and drink, Richard Partington entered.

"What brings you?" Robin asked. "Not bad news, I hope."

Richard shook his head sadly. "As bad as it can be," he said. "The king has sent his men to arrest you. Two bands of men are not far behind."

Robin put his hand on the youth's shoulder. "This is the second time you have saved my life," he said. "When the time comes, you will be rewarded handsomely. As for the Bishop of Hereford who has turned the king against me, I will deal with him as well." He chuckled aloud and turned to his men. "We will go separate ways to Sherwood," he said. "I will meet you there."

The men parted company. Little John, Will, and Allan went one way while Robin went the other. Richard Partington returned to the queen to tell her that Robin was safe, at least for now.

When the king's guards arrived, the innkeeper sent them in the wrong direction.

Little John, Will, and Alan walked steadily until they reached the greenwood and safety. Robin was not as lucky.

"This is the second time you have saved my life."

Robin walked for days until, at last, he felt safe. Sherwood was close by. Unfortunately, the king's guards discovered they were chasing shadows and turned back onto the right path. They sent word to the Sheriff of Nottingham whose men joined the search.

Robin sat in a quiet glen resting his feet. A bird whistled its song and he answered it. The bird's gay tune suddenly changed to the sizzle of an arrow in flight, followed by a dozen more. The king's men had found Robin.

Robin leaped to his feet. He was outnumbered so he chose to run. He ran as fast as he could as arrows pelted the path behind him like drops of deadly rain. After many miles, he was safe again. Each time he came upon a party of the king's men or the sheriff's men, he hid until they passed. At last he was close enough to Sherwood Forest to breath easily.

A man approached on the path. It was the noble knight, Sir Richard of the Lea, a friend. "What good fortune to find a man I trust," Robin exclaimed. He told his story to Sir Richard.

"I know the danger you are in, Robin," Sir Richard said. "The king's and sheriff's men have set traps on every path. I would take you to my castle, but even there your days would be numbered. Your only hope is to ask the queen for her protection. Otherwise you are doomed."

Robin knew his friend spoke the truth. Without a word, the two set out for London Town to see the queen.

Sir Richard of the Lea
approached Robin.

The queen was in her garden when Robin arrived. "My poor fellow," she said with alarm, "don't you know the king has sent his guard after you?"

"I do, your majesty," Robin replied. "I have come to ask for your mercy to save my life."

The queen was embarrassed that her first promise of safety had been broken, though it was not her fault. "I promise you again I will give you my protection," she said. She quickly left the room. After a long while she returned. Her face was red as if she had been in a heated discussion. But her eyes were calm. "I have spoken with the king and he has promised your safe return to Sherwood. He will send his own man with you to see that nobody arrests you. I hope this has taught you a lesson, Robin. I hope you have learned to be more honest in what you do, and I hope you will not be so bold in seeking adventure. You have escaped the lion's wrath by a miracle, but you may not be so lucky again." With that she left the room and was gone.

The king was good to his word. With the king's page in his company, Robin returned safely to Sherwood.

11 KING RICHARD COMES TO SHERWOOD FOREST

A long time passed and many changes came to England. King Henry died and good King Richard returned from the Crusades and took the throne. But Robin and his men lived as before because they did not learn of these things.

One day Robin decided to seek another adventure. He and Little John set out on opposite paths to see what they could find. Robin had walked far from Sherwood when he met a strange man dressed in odd garb. The man was clad in a horsehide garment and covered his head with a leather cowl. He carried a heavy broadsword and in his belt was a double-edged dagger as sharp as a light beam.

"Hello, friend," Robin called to the fierce-looking stranger.

The man said nothing. Instead he pushed back his cowl to reveal a face as ugly as the horse his garment once covered. His eyes were cruel and his lips curled into a sinister snarl. "I am no friend of you or any man," the stranger growled. "Now get out of my way or feel my blade between your ribs."

Guy of Gisbourne was the meanest, most murderous man in the countryside.

"That is not a friendly thing to say," Robin said with a laugh. But he knew the man was serious. "All I ask is to know your name."

"I am Guy of Gisbourne," the stranger snarled. "And I have come at the bidding of the Sheriff of Nottingham to find a scoundrel who lives in these parts by the name of Robin Hood. He I will slay in return for the sheriff's pardon of my past crimes and ten pounds of gold in good measure."

Robin had heard of Guy of Gisbourne. He was the meanest, most murderous man in the countryside. "I have heard of your gentle work," Robin said with a grin. "I believe there is nobody Robin Hood would rather meet than you. I have heard say that he could beat you in any contest for he is clearly the better man."

Guy of Gisbourne stamped his foot heavily on the ground. "I am the better man and I will prove it when we meet," he growled.

Robin stepped closer. "I have heard he is the best archer in the land, but to tell the truth, I am as good and I think I could beat you as readily as he."

"Done!" Guy of Gisbourne shouted. "Put a target on any tree you choose and I will best you here and now."

Robin cut a small stick no thicker than his thumb with his knife. He walked deep into the woods and stuck it into a crack of a tree over 250 feet away. He returned with a grin. "There is your target, gentle Guy of Gisbourne," he said. "Hit it at your pleasure."

Guy of Gisbourne snarled. "No man could hit that," he said, "not even the devil himself."

"You will do in the devil's stead," Robin said. "Or do you concede I am the better man?"

Guy of Gisbourne glared savagely at Robin. "Hold that tongue or I will cut it out," he snarled. He drew his bow and shot. He missed the target by a palm's width. His second missed the tree entirely.

"The devil himself has shot and missed," Robin said as he drew his bow. His first shot scraped the edge of the narrow stick, but his second split it down the middle. He threw his bow to the ground and drew his broadsword. "There is your answer to who is the better man, you murderous villain," he cried. "For I am

Robin Hood."

Guy of Gisbourne pulled his own sword from his belt and raised it high. "I have come to kill you and now I will," he said.

The forest rang with the harsh sound of blade against blade. Each man thrust and parried, but Robin steadily gained ground. His blade nipped at Guy of Gisbourne, enraging him to blind fury. There was never another fight like it in the history of Sherwood Forest. The men danced back and forth over the green grass until it was trampled flat. Suddenly Robin's heel caught on an exposed tree root. He fell on his back to the ground.

"Prepare to die," Guy of Gisbourne shouted. He brought his sword down with a force that would have split a stone.

Robin grabbed at the falling blade. It cut his hand but it was enough to deflect it. The sword plunged into the earth. Robin rolled sideways and leaped to his feet. Now he was on the verge of victory.

Guy of Gisbourne knew it was soon over. He fell back like a cowering dog as Robin's keen blade darted forward. The evil murderer dropped to the ground and would never rise again.

Robin hurried back to Sherwood. He was not happy to have killed a second time, even though the man was a murderous villain.

Not long after, all of Nottinghamshire was excited to hear that King Richard was coming for a visit and would be the guest of the sheriff. The town prepared for the great occasion. Arches were built over the streets and garlands of flowers and banners of colorful silk were draped over them. Flags were hung wherever there was room and a fine throne was built for the king who was greatly loved by his subjects.

The momentous day arrived. The town was packed with people from every corner of the county. Large numbers of the sheriff's men joined the crowd that lined the streets to see the king. Also in the crowd, dressed in bright Lincoln green, were scores of stout yeomen whose clothes were perfumed by the clean air of Sherwood Forest. One, as tall and broad as a young oak tree, wore a friar's robe.

A murmur went up that grew to a roar.

The momentous day arrived.

Bugles sounded and the crowd fell still. A band of musicians entered the street followed by a gallant troop of men armed with lances and broadswords. Behind them were 100 noble knights riding proud horses covered with colorful silks. The knights' armor sparkled in the bright sun. Barons and nobles walked in their trail, each dressed in fine velvet and silk and adorned with gold ornaments and chains. Another mass of armed men followed, and after them pranced a troop of horses bearing elegant riders with plumed hats carrying swords. Behind this rich parade came two riders, side by side. One, the Sheriff of Nottingham, was dressed in garments as elegant as the nobles who preceded him. The man next to him, taller by more than a head,

This was King Richard.

was dressed simply in a light blue tunic of fine cloth. His hair and beard were as yellow as newly spun gold and his blue eyes matched the sky. Around his neck was a heavy gold chain bearing a jeweled seal. This was King Richard.

The king turned to the sheriff. "By my soul, I have never seen such tall friars as you have in Nottingham, Sheriff," he said. He gestured at the towering robed man in the milling crowd.

The sheriff's face turned white. He recognized Little John at once. Next to Little John stood Robin Hood, Will Scarlet, Will Stutely, Allan-a-Dale, Friar Tuck, and others of the band. The sheriff said nothing but rode on, alarmed that Robin was so daring that he would show himself in Nottingham.

That night, after the events in his honor were over and the king had retired to his lodgings, he spoke to his friends who had accompanied him. "I have heard a lot of talk of

The king and his escorts disguised themselves in black robes.

this Robin Hood fellow," he said. "He has bested the sheriff more than once, and has even taken gold from our friend the Bishop of Hereford." The king laughed aloud. "I daresay, he would take gold from us if it served his purpose." He put his hand to his brow. "I would like to meet this outlaw if I could."

Sir Hubert of Bingham spoke up with a grin on his lips. "I can arrange that, sire," he said. "And a banquet feast with the man as well."

"Done," the king said. "See to it."

The next day the king and seven of his escorts dressed themselves in the black robes of the Order of Black Friars. "This disguise will get us to the banquet, I promise," Sir Hubert

Robin stepped from behind a tree.

said.

The king laughed. He hid some gold in the lining of his robe. "I like this adventure," he said. "Let us be off."

The seven rode straight to Sherwood Forest. The ride was long and when they were deep in the woods, the king halted the band. "I have a great thirst," he said. "I would give 50 gold pounds for something to quench it."

No sooner were the words said than a tall fellow with yellow hair and beard stepped from behind a tree. "If your word is as good as your gold, I will take you to a certain inn that I know of where you can feast and drink to your heart's content," he said. He immediately put a silver bugle horn to his lips and blew three short blasts. Instantly a band of Lincoln green-clad yeomen appeared from the forest.

"Take my purse but do not touch me."

114

The king, his face hidden beneath his friar's cowl, looked at the armed men surrounding him. "Have you no respect for holy men, my roguish fellow?" he asked.

Robin laughed aloud. "Not a penny's worth," he said. "We have learned that rich friars are not holy. And, it's true some call me a rogue, but others use my true name which is Robin Hood."

"I have heard of you," the king said. "Now let us get on our way."

"Not before I have inspected your purse," Robin replied. "No stranger passes through Sherwood who is not made an honored guest at our banquet, even though he must pay for the honor."

The king held out his purse. "Take my purse but do not touch me," he said.

"Ho!" Robin crowed. "And who do you think you are, the king of England?" His merry men roared with laughter.

Robin counted the money in the purse. It contained 100 pounds of gold money. He put 50 in his own purse and gave the rest back. "Keep one half as a reminder that rogues such as we are not what we seem," he said.

Robin's men led the black-robed riders to their glade beneath the mighty oak. A grand banquet was spread and soon the woods rang with laughter and song. Robin leaped into the

midst of the revelry with his cup raised high. "I offer a toast to our good King Richard and pledge our everlasting loyalty to him." The merry band of men jumped to their feet and pledged a roaring toast to the king, though none knew the king was their guest.

After the banquet, the guests were entertained with feats of archery by Robin's men. Each one impressed the king with their skill. When it came Robin's turn to shoot, the woods turned silent. His first arrow flew straight to the center of the target. His second came to a rest alongside it.

The king turned to the robed Sir Hubert at his side. "I would give a fortune to have this fellow in my guard," he whispered.

Robin took aim for his final shot. The arrow had a torn feather and missed the target completely. The troop of men roared with laughter. They had never seen Robin miss in all their days together. Robin was furious. "I had a bad arrow," he protested.

Will Scarlet stepped forward. "Your chance was as fair as the rest, dear uncle," he said. Then, with a sly grin he said, "And now I would like to make even the fight we had so long ago when you thrashed me soundly."

Again Robin protested. "I am king in these woods," he said, "and you may not raise your hand against me." He turned to the black-robed priest. "But I will be glad to let this holy father get his money back. What do you say to a fair fight, friar? If you can tumble me to the ground, you earn your money and your freedom. But if I win, I will take your last penny."

"I had a bad arrow," Robin said.

117

The king's blow knocked Robin to the ground.

"Done!" King Richard said. He quickly rolled up his sleeves and stepped forward. Robin's men stared at the friar's arms. They were as tough and sinewy as an oak branch. The king raised one hand and swung it forward as if throwing a stone. The blow caught Robin on the ear and knocked him to the ground as easily as if he were a stalk of dry corn.

Robin's men laughed louder still as Robin staggered to his feet. He shook his head. "Give this good friar his money," he said. "He has beat me like no other man ever."

Will Scarlet counted out the money which the friar returned to his own purse. Before the laughter died down, a shout came from the woods. Little John, Sir Richard of Lea, and a group of Robin's men dashed into the glade.

"King Richard has left Nottingham," Sir Richard said to Robin. "Quickly take your men and hide until the danger has passed." Then he spied the strangers dressed in black robes. Suddenly his face turned scarlet. He knew in an instant who the tall friar was. The knight quickly dropped to his knee and bowed to his king.

King Richard threw back his cowl. Everyone recognized him at once and each man dropped to his knee in salute.

"How is it you would shelter this outlaw, Sir Richard of the Lea?" King Richard asked.

"An outlaw he may be," Sir Richard replied, "but he has done more good than harm and knows justice better than any man. I owe him my own life. It would be an honor to shelter him."

The king knew very well of Robin's feats. He looked over the sea of kneeling knights and yeomen. "Rise all of you," he said. "You have my pardon." Then he beckoned to Robin to join him. "Your past deeds are forgiven. They are not to be taken lightly, but I now overlook them. However, I cannot let you roam as an outlaw. I have heard you pledge your life to me, Robin Hood. I take you at your word. Come with me to London where you shall enter my service and be at my side. We will take with us Little John and Will Scarlet and Allan-a-Dale, too. The rest of your band is also pardoned.

Robin pledges himself to the king's service.

They will be made royal rangers whose duty is
to protect my forests and herds. Now let us
continue this feast for today is a most joyous
occasion for all."

The merry men threw their hats into the
air with a shout that could be heard in
Nottingham Town and returned to the banquet
with more gusto than ever before.

The next morning Robin and his men and
the King and his men marched to Nottingham.
The sheriff was dumbfounded to see Robin at
the side of the king but there was nothing he
could do.

Robin's merry band of men gathered
around Robin, Will Scarlet, Little John, and

Allan-a-Dale. All shook hands heartily. Robin pledged to return often. Then Robin, Will, Little John, and Allan mounted their horses and rode away in the service of the king.

12 ROBIN SHOOTS HIS LAST ARROW

Robin did not return to Sherwood Forest for many years. Little John eventually left the king's service to live in Nottingham and Will Scarlet returned to his home. Robin's yeomen worked as rangers and did well, but Robin and Allan-a-Dale stayed with the king.

King Richard favored Robin and soon made him chief of all his men. Robin was so faithful and loyal, that after a few years, the king made him the Earl of Huntington, a true noble.

Robin fought well for his lionhearted king in many wars. Then, sadly, King Richard was slain in battle and his throne taken by John.

One gentle spring day as Robin roamed the forests near the king's castle, a deep longing came over him to return to Sherwood. He asked the king's permission and it was granted, but only for three days after which he must return.

Robin and Allan-a-Dale and his wife, fair Ellen, rode to Sherwood. Robin recognized each stone in the path and every tree. He saw the scar where his arrow had struck when he once missed a deer and remembered old times that were good and merry. When they came to the giant oak they fell silent. It was just as it had been years earlier, but now there was no band of men feasting beneath its mighty boughs. Robin's eyes filled with salty tears as memories of those long-ago days returned. Out of habit, he took his old silver bugle horn from his belt and blew three short blasts.

Suddenly the woods filled with the sound of running feet. Little John, who happened to be walking nearby, heard the sweet note and raced to the glen. A small band of rangers, once Robin's trusted men, also heard the sound. They, too, came running. Then another band and another. Will Stutely, leading a squad of rangers, followed. Will threw his arms around Robin and wept openly. Soon the woods were filled with laughter and happy shouts as the old friends hugged and cried for joy.

Robin gazed at the troop of adoring friends and at that instant vowed never again to leave. "I am no longer Earl of Huntington," he declared, "I am Robin Hood, the yeoman!"

The band of men roared their approval and in no time set a feast fit for a king, just like old times.

When King John heard the news that Robin Hood had returned to Sherwood for good, he vowed he would not rest until he had him back, dead or alive. Sir William Dale had

The old friends hugged and cried for joy.

no love for Robin and the king knew it. King John appointed him head of an army of men whose job was to find Robin.

The king's men searched for days. At last they came upon Robin and his yeomen. Robin no longer wanted to fight for he had had his fill in wars fighting for King Richard. But Sir William sent his men against him and a bloody battle followed. The first to fall was the Sheriff of Nottingham who had eagerly joined in the hunt. Other men fell until at last, beaten and wounded, Sir William raced for safety.

Robin was deeply saddened by this battle. It had been a fair fight, but he brooded over the killing. Soon a deep fever seized him. He grew sick and weak. Fearing for his life, Little John took Robin to a nunnery to be cared for by Robin's own cousin who was the prioress in charge. King Richard had given her the job as a reward out of his admiration for Robin. But the prioress was greedy and sought to find favor with King John. She did not tell anyone her true feelings.

When Robin was laid on a bed in the nunnery, the prioress prepared to bleed him, which was the treatment for a fever at that time. Instead of pricking a small vein, she cut deep into Robin's arm so that the blood flowed fast and free. Pleased with her ill deed, she left the room, locking the door behind her.

Robin lay helpless on his bed all day. The life slowly ran from his arm. Late that evening, Little John grew alarmed. He ran to the room and pounded on the door. When it would not budge, he threw a huge stone against it and it burst open. When he saw his master, he shouted for help.

The prioress came at once. Now she was more fearful of Little John and she quickly bandaged Robin's arm. Little John relaxed. "You will be roaming the woods with me by tomorrow morning," he said to Robin.

But Robin knew the truth. "I will never roam the woods again," he said slowly. Little John dropped to Robin's bedside. There he sat in silence until the sun sank to the edge of the horizon. Robin gazed out the window. "Bring me my bow," he said faintly. "I long to shoot it one more time."

Robin wrapped his fingers lovingly around the bow.

Little John argued, but soon realized it was no use. Reluctantly, he brought Robin's bow to the bed. He handed it and an arrow to his master. Robin wrapped his fingers lovingly around the bow. He carefully nocked an arrow to the string. "Where this arrow lands, there shall be my grave," he said. He sat upright with a great effort. Suddenly his old strength seemed to return. He drew the bow as he had in old times and let the arrow fly. It soared like a bird out the window. With it went Robin's life.

Robin fell back into Little John's arms. Little John held his beloved master for a long while. Then he laid him gently down on the bed. He folded Robin's hands across his silent breast and covered his face with a white linen. He got up and left the room without saying a word.

And so it was that Robin Hood died. He was laid to rest where his arrow fell but his spirit lives forever in these tales of great adventure.